EXPLORING THE UNITED KINGDOM

LET'S GO TO... ENGLAND

WRITTEN BY NOAH LEATHERLAND

© This edition published in 2026.
First published in 2024.
BookLife Publishing Ltd.
King's Lynn, Norfolk
PE30 2HN, UK

A catalogue record for this book is available from the British Library.

ISBN: 978-1-80505-612-6

Written by:
Noah Leatherland

Edited by:
Elise Carraway

Designed by:
Amelia Harris

FSC
www.fsc.org
MIX
Paper | Supporting
responsible forestry
FSC® C011748

CONTENTS

WORDS THAT LOOK LIKE THIS CAN BE FOUND IN THE GLOSSARY ON PAGE 24.

WELCOME TO THE UNITED KINGDOM

The United Kingdom might look small on a world map. However, there is so much to explore around its four countries. The islands of the United Kingdom are packed with history and culture.

SCOTLAND

ENGLAND

NORTHERN IRELAND

WALES

ENGLAND, WALES, SCOTLAND AND NORTHERN IRELAND ARE PART OF THE UNITED KINGDOM.

ENGLAND

A long time ago, England was made up of lots of small kingdoms. It became one country in the year 927 when one king brought them all together. Since then, it has changed a lot...

BUTTERMERE

LONDON

London is England's capital city. A capital city is usually a country's most important city. London is the home of the royal family. They have lived there in Buckingham Palace for many years.

BUCKINGHAM PALACE

London is also important because it is where the Houses of Parliament are found. Politicians from all over the United Kingdom come to the Houses of Parliament to decide on how the countries are run.

THE HOUSES OF PARLIAMENT

23 BUS
LONDON

THE WHITE CLIFFS OF
DOVER

The White Cliffs of Dover are among the most famous <u>natural</u> sights in England. They stretch along the south coast of the country. The cliffs are made of chalk, which gives them their white colour.

The English Channel is the stretch of sea between the United Kingdom and France. On a clear day, the White Cliffs of Dover can be seen all the way from France!

THE WHITE CLIFFS OF DOVER

THE ENGLISH CHANNEL

FRANCE

SIGHTS TO SEE

The Angel of the North is a huge statue. For some people, it reminds them of the coal <u>mines</u> that used to run in that area. For others, it is a <u>symbol</u> of hope.

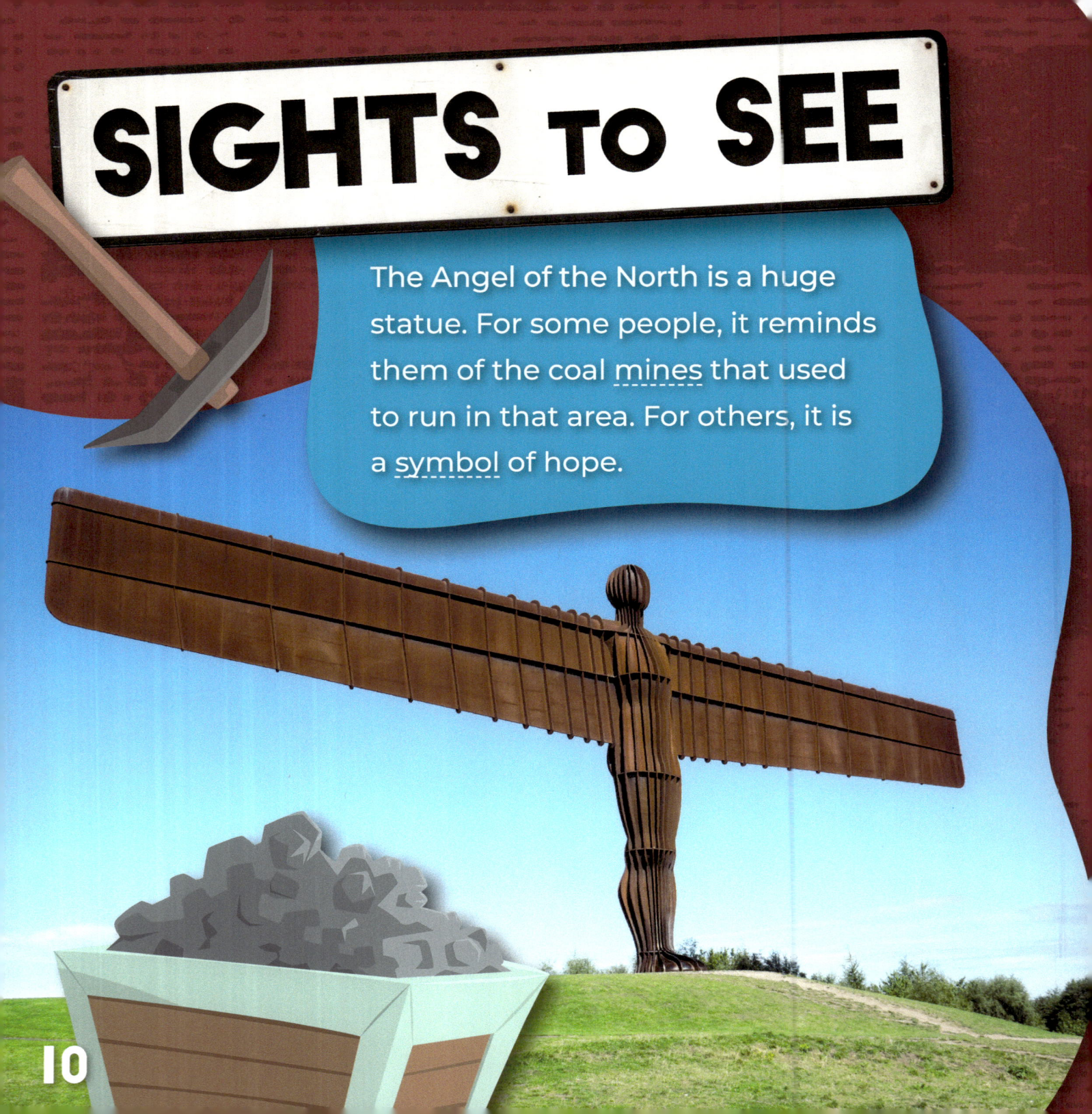

Stonehenge was first built over 5,000 years ago. It is thought that Stonehenge was built to mark the summer and winter solstices. Solstices mark the longest and shortest days of the year.

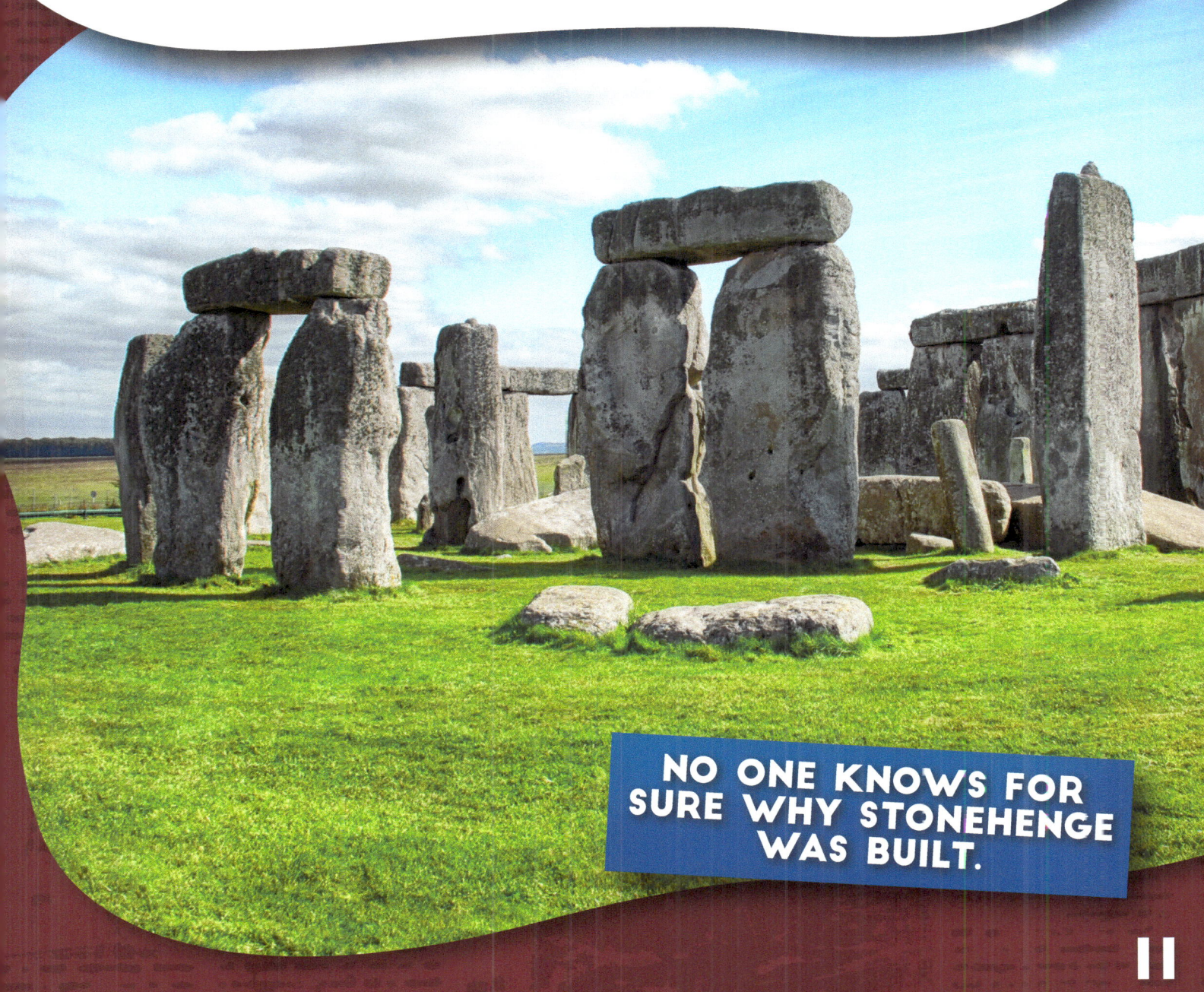

NO ONE KNOWS FOR SURE WHY STONEHENGE WAS BUILT.

FISH AND CHIPS

Fish and chips is a popular dish in England. Normally, the fish is covered in batter and deep fried to make it crispy. People might add salt and vinegar, peas and curry sauce to their dish.

Sometimes, people eat the pieces of batter that fall off while the fish is cooking. In some places, these pieces are called 'scraps'. In other places, they are 'scrumps'. Sometimes, they are just called 'bits'.

A FISH AND CHIP SHOP IS SOMETIMES CALLED A 'CHIPPY'.

THE ENGLISH
ROSE

In the 1400s, England was split into two sides. The two sides went to war with each other. One side used a red rose as its symbol and the other used a white rose.

THE TUDOR ROSE ON A COIN

After the war, the two sides came together and made a new symbol. It was a red and white rose called the Tudor Rose. It is now the national flower of England.

THE ENGLISH
LION

Even though they are not naturally found in England, lions have become a national symbol. It all started hundreds of years ago when the old English kings wanted the country to look strong.

A LION STATUE IN TRAFALGAR SQUARE, LONDON

Old Red Lion

Circa 1610

Lions are used as symbols of strength and bravery. All over the country, lions can be found on buildings, signs and badges. You cannot go far in England without seeing some sort of lion!

CRICKET

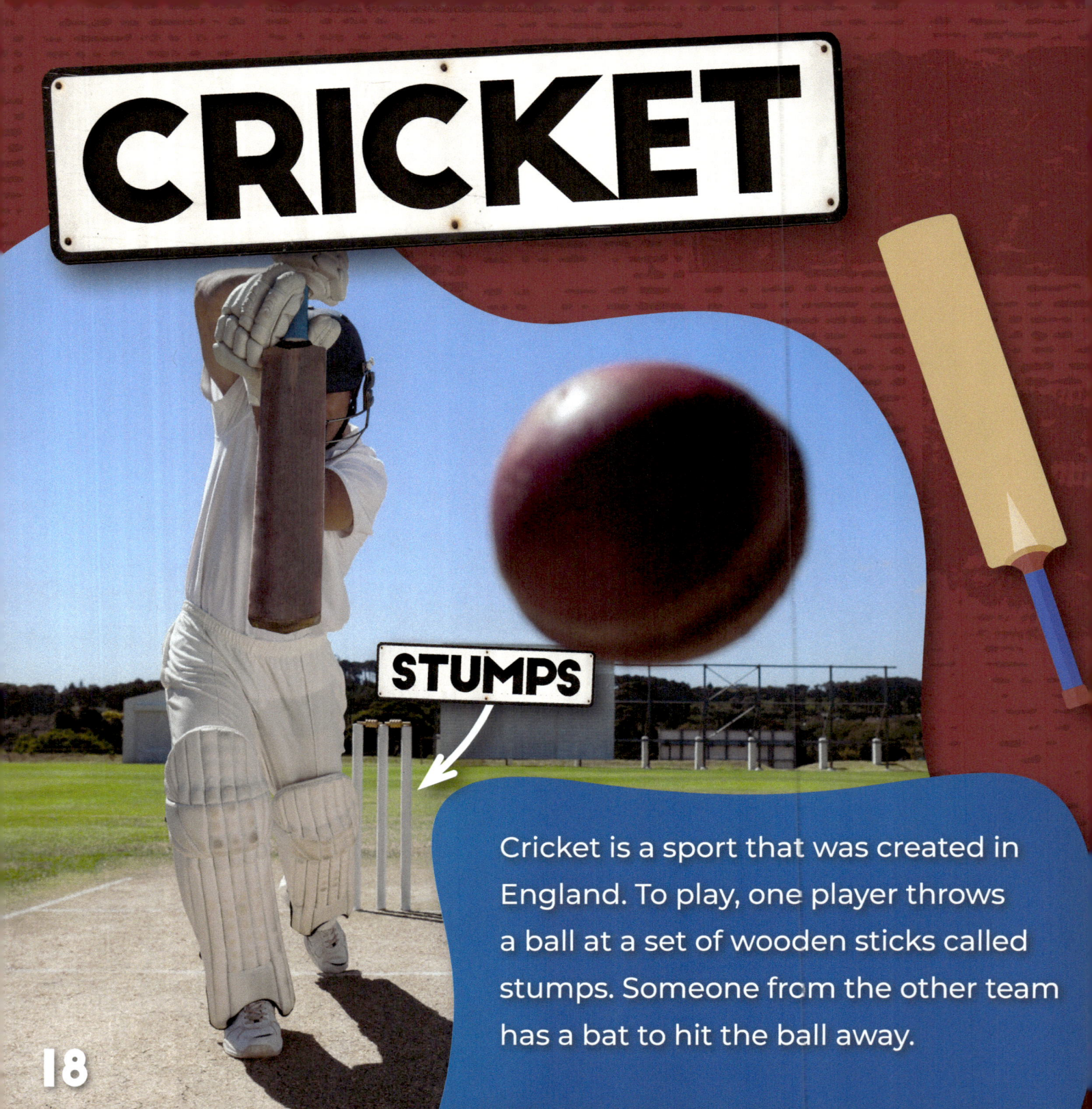

STUMPS

Cricket is a sport that was created in England. To play, one player throws a ball at a set of wooden sticks called stumps. Someone from the other team has a bat to hit the ball away.

Lord's Cricket Ground in London is known as the 'Home of Cricket'. It was first opened all the way back in 1814. Today, it can seat over 30,000 cricket fans.

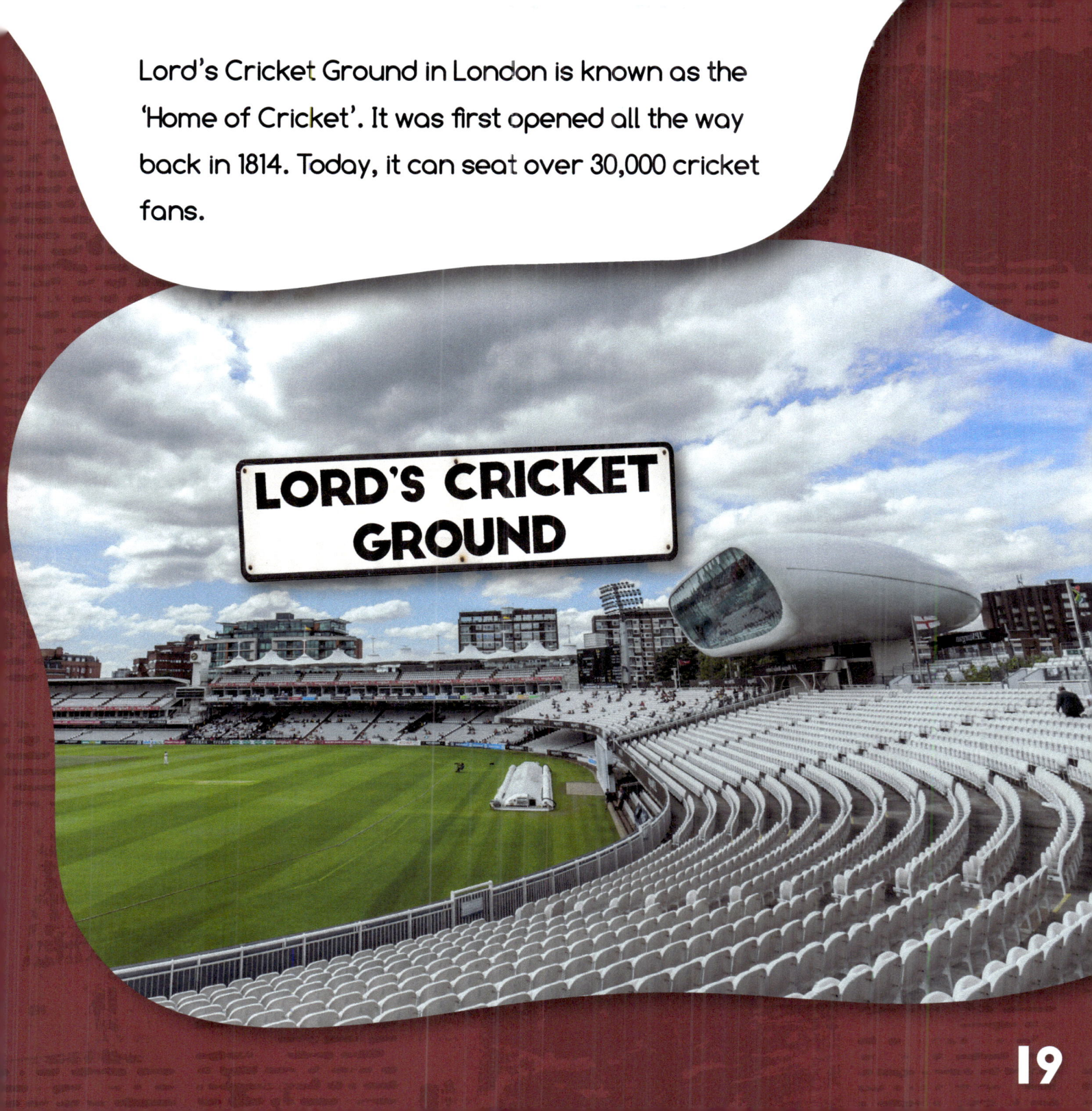

LORD'S CRICKET GROUND

BONFIRE NIGHT

GUY FAWKES

In 1605, Guy Fawkes planned to blow up the Houses of Parliament. He was caught before he could do it. The country has celebrated that Guy Fawkes's plan failed every 5th of November since then.

THE HOUSES OF PARLIAMENT

The celebration has become known as Bonfire Night. As part of the tradition, people all over the country make big fires called bonfires and set off lots of fireworks.

EXPLORING THE UNITED KINGDOM

You have only just started exploring England! There is so much more you can find out about the people, the places and the culture. What else do you want to discover?

England is just one part of the United Kingdom. There are three other countries in the kingdom that have just as much culture and history for you to explore! Where will you go next?

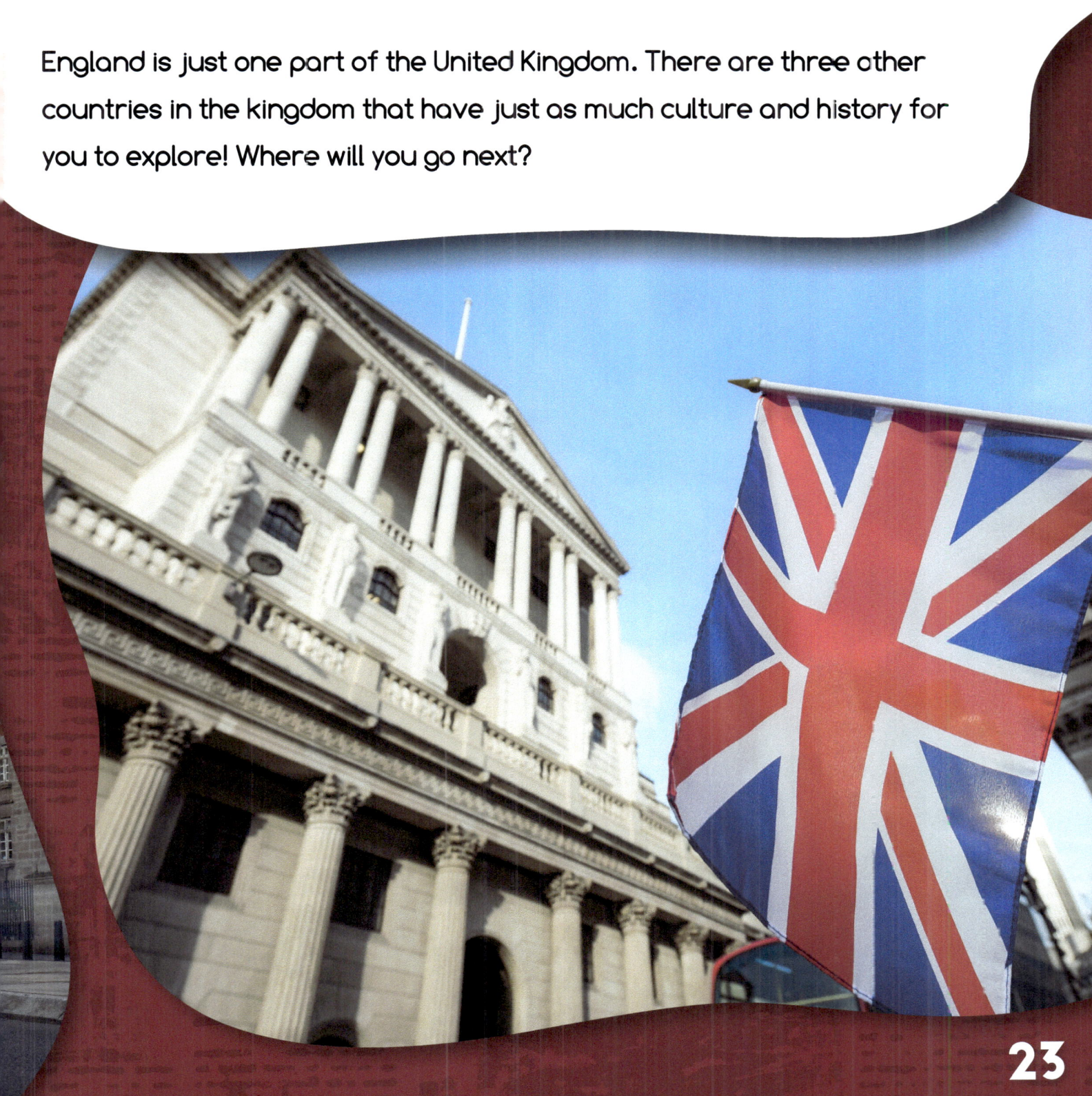

GLOSSARY

CULTURE — the traditions, ideas and ways of life of a group of people

MINES — places where useful rocks are taken out of the ground

NATIONAL — to do with things that are shared by people in a country

NATURAL — found in nature and not made by people

POLITICIANS — people involved with making important decisions for a country

ROYAL FAMILY — the family of the king or queen

SYMBOL — a thing that is used as a sign of something else

TRADITION — a belief or action that is passed down between people over time

INDEX